I GOT THIS

Dr. Courtney A. Griffin

Copyright © 2024 Dr. Courtney A. Griffin

All rights reserved.

ISBN: 979-8-9987439-1-7

DEDICATION

To my mommy, who instilled me, I got this. And for all the Black girls debating on if you do, you got this!

TABLE OF CONTENTS

1. Motivational   1
2. Educational   15
3. Evolving   45
4. Self-Love   77
5. Future Self   10

HOW TO USE THIS BOOK

You can read this book in order, or feel free to skip ahead to a chapter that speaks to you. Each chapter includes an affirmation for the week on the left side. I've chosen weekly affirmations so you can say them every day for 7 days. Make sure to speak the affirmation to yourself in the mirror every morning before leaving the house.

On the right side, you'll find a message from me explaining why each affirmation is important and how it will help you on your life journey. If anyone asks why you're saying these affirmations, simply point them to the right page—that's your answer.

MOTIVATIONAL

I got this.

I GOT THIS

Title of the book and something my mom told me often. I didn't always believe it, but when she told me it gave me the confidence to finish, or heck start whatever it was.

I am more than enough.

We often think whatever we're doing is enough, that we could or should be doing more. More often we need to appreciate the journey and where we are.

I am my ancestors' wildest dreams.

Believe it or not, your ancestors dreamed this life for you! You're exactly who they wanted you to be. They fought for this for you. Kudos on a job well done.

I GOT THIS

I'm living out my ancestors' wildest dreams.

The experiences you're having, the people you've met, the places you're traveling your ancestors wished they could. Again, congratulations on a job well done.

Failure isn't an option

Regardless of how hard things seem, you can and will succeed. You may just have to work a little differently or a little harder, but you can and will succeed.

I GOT THIS

My contributions are valid.

People want to hear what you gave to say! You're smart, you bring a lot to the table share it. Even if you're not quite comfortable, yet.

I GOT THIS

EDUCATIONAL

I belong here.

You belong at your institution. They're grateful to have you. You may or may not have a number or peers or professors that look like you but that doesn't impact you and your worth. You deserve to be exactly where you are.

I GOT THIS

I will graduate on time.

College is not a linear journey. It looks different and feels different for everyone. If you want to graduate "on time" whatever that means for you. Speak it now. Write it down. Envision yourself walking across the stage that year. Envision your outfit, your shoes. Everything.

I GOT THIS

I will go to office hours.

Professors are here for you! Go to their office. Talk to them. You never know what will come from having a strong relationship with them. Could be mentorship, an internship a better grade, possibilities are endless.

I have a good relationship with my professors.

Professors are just people. They may look different. They may have years of experience, and yes, they give you a grade but they're just people. Go talk to them! Ask for help. Find out who they know. What do they need help with it? It'll help you in the long run! I promise.

I GOT THIS

I am more than a bad grade.

I GOT THIS

Bad grades happen. They teach us what we do know. Next time, you'll do better. This feeling and this grade is only temporary.

I'm prepared and ready for this exam

I GOT THIS

Say this one before an exam! You got this! You've studied; you've went to office hours. You're ready, you're prepared, and you'll do great.

I GOT THIS

I'm prepared for this!

You've committed to going to college and gaining a degree therefore you're prepared. You have the tools you need, and if you don't you know who to go to it to find it.

I GOT THIS

My work is good enough.

Your work doesn't have to be perfect, but it does have to be complete. As long as you put your all into it, it's good enough. Submit it, and let it go!

I GOT THIS

I'm going to get a great internship

Girl! You've learned an immense amount. Making great connections. Companies would love to have you on their team.

I GOT THIS

I bring my full self—my culture, my voice, and my brilliance—to this college environment.

Regardless of what the media tries to portray, we bring valuable knowledge, skills and experience to the college environment. They are grateful to have us. Don't dim yourself to fit into the mold. Be yourself. Always. It's the best version of you. It isn't too much. I promise.

I GOT THIS

I'm prepared for this!

You've committed to going to college and gaining a degree therefore you're prepared. You have the tools you need, and if you don't you know who to go to it to find it.

I have the ability to be social on campus.

If you're an introvert or do not think being social is important this one is for you. Research tells us that students who are more active on campus are more likely to succeed. You want to succeed, so be active, be social. It'll enhance your college experience, and you never know who you'll meet and who you'll still be friends with in 29 years.

I GOT THIS

I'm a good test taker!

Too often as Black women and girls are our test taking skills are not emphasized enough. We have to remind ourselves that yes, we are good test takers. Standardized test, final exams, all of it. We have it in us to tackle it.

I GOT THIS

This project is fire!

Whether it is or isn't. Submit it like it is. As long as you put actual effort into it, own it. That project is fire!

I GOT THIS

EVOLVING

I am assertive and soft.

I struggle with this one too! We can say what we mean without being aggressive. We can also be soft without being walked over. You can do both. They're both required at different times, for different situations.

I GOT THIS

I don't have to do anything I don't want to.

You may encounter an immense amount of peer pressure in college. Do not succumb to it. Don't succumb to the pressure of your parents, of your peers, of anyone. This time is for you! Do what you want, and nothing more or nothing less.

I speak slowly and intentionally.

Too often did I speak fast to hurry up and get it over with. I don't want that for you. Slow down. People want to hear what you have to say. Do it with intention. Use your word choice wisely.

I GOT THIS

I can only control what I can control and that's okay.

I GOT THIS

This one is simple. Too often do we try to control more than we are able. We cannot control everything. There are a handful of things we cannot control, but the things we can control. You do a great job! Keep it up. Do not over think it.

I GOT THIS

I can ask for help.

Too often do college students feel as if they must figure everything out themselves. That could not be the furthest thing from the truth. You can ask for help. Ask your parent, friends, professors, and mentors. They all should be there to help you and if by chance they say no, it's fine. Move on to the next person. They'll be willing to help you.

I GOT THIS

My finances will stretch.

Managing your own finances is tough. Especially if you do not have enough to start with. College and finances can be stressful. However, it's only temporary. Be strategic; you can make your funds stretch.

I GOT THIS

My instinct is always right.

Do not overthink it. Your intuition will not steer you wrong. If it seems odd, it's probably not for you. If it seems easy and you're excited, it's probably for you!

I GOT THIS

I trust my gut.

Your gut doesn't lie. Some even say your gut is your ancestors speaking to you. Listen to it. Don't fight it. Embrace it. Again, do not over think.

I can say no.

I GOT THIS

Do it! Say no, and don't feel guilty about it! We know no is a complete sentence. Whomever doesn't like it will get over it.

I GOT THIS

I forgive those who have wronged me.

You will encounter a number of people along your collegiate journey. Some may be for you; some will be against you. You do not have to use your energy holding a grudge against someone. You also do not have to forget how they wronged you. You can, however, forgive them and use your energy elsewhere. Remember, this doesn't mean let them walk over you. It just means don't harp on it. Move on.

I have no desire to please everyone.

No one expects you to, please everyone. It's impossible. There are decisions you may make that everyone may not approve of. That's okay. What matters most is that you're happy and proud of the decision you've made. Because trying to please everyone will not please you and you matter most!

I learn from my mistakes.

This is your fist time on your own, you're going to do a few things wrong. It's okay! There was a lesson there.

I stand up for myself.

I know it can be uncomfortable to stand up for yourself, but it'll be worth it, and you'll feel so empowered after. Do not let people walk over you, mispronounce your name, speak down to you or anything else you don't like. Stand up to them, standup for yourself, the more you do it. The easier it'll become.

I GOT THIS

I can choose who I call family and not feel guilty about it.

Yes, you know who raised you, but you also know who supports you and encouraged you and they may or may not be the same people. This is the time where you can decide who you like to call family. Who makes you feel welcome, who can you call on for support, who encourages you. You can lean into those people.

I GOT THIS

What is going on at home is out of my control.

I GOT THIS

This one can be difficult to accept. However, it's true, you cannot save everyone and everything going on at home. I'm not telling you to abandon your family and friends. I'm just saying remind yourself that you're enrolled in college to better yourself and your family by way of success. Focus on that. Don't feel guilty about not being able stop and drop your life because things are going on. Of course, be courteous when you tell them you can't.

I GOT THIS

SELF–LOVE

I GOT THIS

I love the life I'm creating.

Girl! This is your life! No one else's, enjoy it! Embrace it! Love it! Even the mistakes, there's a lesson there.

I'm a good person.

Do not let one interaction, one bad though have you questioning your entire existence. You're a good person. We all have bad days, and that's okay. At the core, we have good intentions and don't let anyone convince you otherwise.

My feelings are more important than others.

I GOT THIS

I struggled with this one for a very long time. Not only do your feelings matter, but they're also more important than whosever's feelings you're trying to consider. Trust me, they're not as worried about your feelings as you are about theirs. Put yourself first! Do what makes you feel good, what makes you feel accomplished.

I GOT THIS

I'm a great daughter.

College can be a difficult time between parents and daughters. That's okay! This riff may be temporary or permanent. Regardless, you're figuring out who you are without the influence of your parents. Enjoy the journey. You're a great daughter. You're doing what you should be doing and working to make your parents proud.

I GOT THIS

I'm a great friend.

One argument doesn't make you a bad friend. It makes you someone who spoke your truth. Could you have done it differently? Great possibility. Regardless, you're a great friend. People love hanging with you. And if not, why? What do we need to change?

I GOT THIS

I'm God's favorite.

You may be encountering something's that makes you feel like God has forgotten about you. I can assure you, he has not! You will also have experiences and then know for certain that you are his favorite. Say it believe it. Strengthen your relationship with him.

I am allowed to put myself first and not feel guilty about it.

Keywords here, not feeling guilty about it! You cannot pour from an empty glass. You have to put yourself first in order to accomplish your goals, pour into other people, and to even feel whole. Take time for yourself, you've worked hard. You deserve it. Make time for you.

I GOT THIS

I love life.

Too often are we focused on the future and thinking how great we'll be then. Enjoy this moment. Soak it in. You are great now! You've already accomplished so much.

I GOT THIS

I'm giving myself grace today.

I GOT THIS

Every day is different. Every day will not be perfect. Give yourself grace on a day where you're not feeling the greatest. Do something you enjoy. Meet up with friends. Eat a good meal. Whatever you do, don't beat yourself up. It's okay! It's part of the journey.

I GOT THIS

I matter.

Regardless of how you may feel, how large or small your institution, your relationship with your friends or those at home, you matter. Act like it!

I GOT THIS

My voice matters.

I GOT THIS

Your voice matters. You owe it to yourself and to others to share your thoughts, viewpoints, your voice with others. Take up space.

I'm putting myself first.

I GOT THIS

This is your time to be selfish. You have nothing to worry about but yourself and your coursework. Be selfish. Put yourself, and your feelings first. Who knows when/ if you'll be able to again.

I GOT THIS

I am good enough, just the way I am.

Remind yourself of this often. You are good enough! Regardless of what's going on, you're good enough. You deserve to be at your college/university. You're good enough to run for office, to apply for the internship, apply for the scholarship, apply for the job. You're good enough! Of course there is always room to improve, but right now, you're perfect. You also do not need validation from anyone else. Don't sleep on yourself.

I trust myself.

I GOT THIS

You have more knowledge than you truly give yourself credit for. Trust yourself to make decisions. You can of course gain feedback, but at the end of the day you always going to have you. So, trust yourself.

I GOT THIS

I GOT THIS

FUTURE SELF

I GOT THIS

I'm making my family proud.

This is important to many children. What am I doing? Does my family approve? Are they proud? I assure you, they're proud! They're singing your praises to their friend/coworker any chance they get. Keep doing things to make them proud, you got this!

I GOT THIS

I am in control of my future.

I GOT THIS

Only you (and God) have the ability to impact what your future looks like. Start envisioning it now. Make it a reality. You can do it. You don't need anyone else to make your future what you want it to be.

I GOT THIS

I will graduate on time.

This looks different for everyone. What started as a 4-year journey for me with 1 degree ended as a 5-year journey with 2 degrees. Whatever your goal is, is possible! And your goal may change overtime. Speak whatever your timeline is into existence. Write it down, make it real. You can do it, again… you got this!

I GOT THIS

A fulfilling high-paying job is waiting for me at the graduation finish line.

I GOT THIS

We attend college for a good job/career, right? Let's speak your fulfilling, high-paying job into existence. Believe it. Envision it. What is it? How does it make u feel? What will you wear on your first day? As you step into this new chapter of your life, never forget who you are and where you come from. College will challenge you, grow you, and stretch you—but you are more than ready.

Come back to these affirmations whenever you need a reminder of your brilliance, your purpose, and your power. Keep speaking life over yourself, even on the hard days. Especially on the hard days.

You don't have to have it all figured out. Just keep showing up as your full, authentic self—because that's more than enough.

And when the world tries to make you doubt it, remember this:
You got this. You always have.

ABOUT THE AUTHOR

Dr. Courtney A. Griffin is an educator, mentor, and advocate dedicated to helping young girls—especially Black girls—see their full potential. As the founder of *Black Girls College Guide* and a College Success Mentor she has supported hundreds of students on their path to confidence, college, and beyond.

She is the author of *I'm Not Just Pretty, I'm Smart Too*, a book of affirmations for school-aged girls, and *You Got This: A Book of Affirmations for College-Bound Black Girls*, both created to uplift, inspire, and remind young Black girls of their power at every stage of their journey.

With a background in education, higher education leadership, and youth mentorship, her passion lies in creating spaces where girls feel seen, heard, and celebrated for their brilliance. She believes that affirmations are more than just words—they're tools for transformation.

Through her writing, programs, and public speaking, she continues her mission of building up the next generation of powerful, purpose-filled girls who know their worth and walk boldly in it every day.

www.ingramcontent.com/pod-product-compliance
Lightning Source LLC
Chambersburg PA
CBHW050526100526
44581CB00009B/150/J